TUNDRA

MICHAEL GEORGE

CREATIVE EDUCATION

Designed by Rita Marshall
with the help of Thomas Lawton

Published by Creative Education
123 South Broad Street,
Mankato, Minnesota 56001
Creative Education is an imprint
of Creative Education, Inc.

Photography by Peter Arnold, Inc.
(N. Rosing), Bryan & Cherry
Alexander, Comstock (Jack Elness,
George D. Lepp, Michael Stuckey),
Rick McIntyre, Boyd Norton, Photo
Researchers (Michael Giannechini,
Dan Guravich), and Tom Stack &
Associates (John Cancalosi, Barbara
von Hoffmann, John Shaw, Robert
Winslow)

Library of Congress
Cataloging-in-Publication Data

George, Michael, 1964–
Tundra / written by Michael
George.
Includes index.
Summary: Describes the location,
climate, and plant and animal life of
the tundras in the Arctic regions.
ISBN 0-88682-601-2
1. Tundras—Arctic regions—
Juvenile literature. [1. Tundras.
2. Arctic regions. 3. Tundra
ecology. 4. Ecology.] 93-18275
GB578.99.G46 1993 CIP
551.4'53—dc20

In Memory of
GEORGE R. PETERSON, SR.

6

The Arctic tundra is a world unlike any other. Flat plains stretch as far as the eye can see. Winters are long, dark, and bitterly cold. Only a few hardy animals struggle to survive. But for a few short months every year, the tundra comes to life with unparalleled brilliance. Summer's mild temperatures and continuous sunshine support a vivid array of plants, animals, birds, and insects, which flourish briefly before succumbing to winter once again.

Greenland: the tundra in summer.

9

The Arctic tundra covers the northernmost land in Europe, Asia, North America, Greenland, and Iceland. It begins where the great northern forests end. Although maps often show a distinct tree line, the forests do not end abruptly; the trees gradually become smaller and farther apart. On the tundra, only a few small trees remain. The tundra's marshy plains extend northward to the shores of the *Arctic Ocean,* the frozen sea that covers the top of the world.

Approaching the tree line in northern Canada.

The tundra's unusual climate is a result of the earth's movement around the sun. Once each year, the earth makes a complete orbit, or circle, around the sun. As the planet makes this annual journey, it is always tilted. For half of the earth's orbit, from March to September, the northern part of the planet is tilted toward the sun. During this period, the tundra is warmed by days of nearly constant sunshine. For the other half of the orbit, from September to March, the northern part of the earth is tilted away from the sun and receives very little sunshine. Winter takes hold of the land.

The midnight sun shines on the thawing tundra.

By October, the temperature is well below freezing and the ground is covered with snow. Each day, the air grows colder and the sunlight hours grow shorter; soon the sun just peeks above the horizon before it sets. Eventually, over much of the tundra, the sun does not rise at all. The land is cloaked in darkness.

﹌

During these dark months, temperatures of 40 or 50 degrees below zero F (minus 40 or 46 degrees C) are common. The cold, dense air creates an area of high atmospheric pressure that does not easily release moisture; thus, it rarely snows on the tundra during this time. From December to March, the sky over the tundra is usually clear. Stars shine brightly, and the northern lights shimmer like pale curtains against the deep black sky. When the air is still, the snowflakes on the ground sparkle like diamonds.

Aurora borealis: the northern lights.

Although winters are long and harsh, the tundra is not without life. A few hardy animals have learned to cope with the cold. One of the most unusual year-round inhabitants of the tundra is the *Musk-Ox*. Musk-oxen are bulky animals with large, curved horns. They have shaggy coats of hair that protect them from the cold. Large herds of musk-oxen live in some of the most desolate areas of the tundra, including the shores of the Arctic Ocean, where darkness lasts for months and the temperature never rises above zero. Even in the coldest weather, musk-oxen do not seek shelter. They roam across barren hilltops, searching for frozen twigs or grass beneath the snow.

Rugged musk-oxen.

The *Arctic Fox* is another animal that can withstand the cold winters on the tundra. Like musk-oxen, arctic foxes have thick, warm coats of fur. Their fur is grayish brown in summer, but turns pure white or blue-gray in the winter. The changing colors blend in with the tundra landscape, helping the foxes avoid their enemies and surprise their prey.

The arctic fox's white fur blends in with its snowy surroundings.

The foxes eat hares, birds, and *Lemmings,* which are small rodents that dig tunnels beneath the snow. When food is hard to find, the arctic fox may follow polar bears or wolves, which sometimes catch animals that are too big for them to eat all by themselves. After a polar bear or wolf has gorged itself, an arctic fox will finish off the remains. This practice is a risky one, however, as both polar bears and wolves have been known to eat arctic foxes.

A lemming looks for food in the summer.

19

A few types of birds spend winters on the tundra. *Ptarmigans* are chickenlike birds that live in the driest areas of the tundra. They feed on tender leaves and berries in the summer, but settle for frozen vegetation after the snow arrives. Short feathers on their feet help them travel in the snow. Like the fur of arctic foxes, ptarmigans' brown feathers turn white in the winter, helping them hide from their enemies.

One of the ptarmigan's worst enemies is the *Snowy Owl,* another bird that lives on the tundra year-round, except during the severest winters when food becomes scarce. Besides ptarmigans, snowy owls eat lemmings as well as arctic hares that are nearly twice their size. During the long days of summer, snowy owls hunt in daylight and at night, unlike most other owls.

Page 18: A willow ptarmigan in winter.
Page 19: By September, the rock ptarmigan's
feathers have begun to turn white.
Inset: Face-to-face with a snowy owl.

20

By the middle of February, the sun has made a welcome return to most of the land, and the tundra's winter inhabitants can sense the promise of spring. But winter loosens its grasp slowly on the tundra. For several more months the land remains frozen. Finally, in May, the snowdrifts begin to melt and the tundra gradually thaws.

❧

Warm sunshine softens the topmost layer of tundra soil. Beneath this thin layer of dirt, however, the ground remains frozen all year long. In some places, this permanently frozen ground, called *Permafrost*, is nearly a mile (1.6 km) deep. Permafrost has a dramatic effect on the tundra. It prevents spring meltwater from seeping into the ground. As a result, although the tundra receives very little precipitation, each spring it becomes a wet, soggy swamp dotted by thousands of lakes and ponds.

Purple saxifrage is the first flower to appear on the flooded tundra.

As summer approaches, days on the tundra gradually grow longer. By the middle of June, the sun just dips below the horizon before it rises. Days later, the sun does not set at all. Throughout much of the tundra, the sun circles above the horizon for days or weeks. Farther north, daylight may last for months. This is why the tundra is often called "the land of the midnight sun."

The arctic sun hangs low on the horizon in northwest Greenland.

Despite the long, sun-drenched days, summers on the tundra are rather cool. In July, the warmest month, the temperature usually does not rise above 50 degrees F (10 degrees C). Occasionally, however, there are warm days on the tundra and even a few that are hot. During a heat wave, some areas may warm up to 80 degrees F (27 degrees C).

Abundant water, continuous sunshine, and mild temperatures transform the once-frozen tundra into a beautiful garden. Grasses, sedges, and mosses carpet the thin, water-soaked soil. The open meadows are blanketed with sprouting leaves and blooming wildflowers.

Like the tundra wildlife, tundra *Plants* have adapted to the climate in several ways. Compared to more familiar vegetation, plants on the tundra are unusually small. Summers are just too short for trees and other plants to grow very tall. With only about eight weeks of summer, it would take more than a century for a tree to grow 3 feet (91 cm) high. Even if the trees could grow faster, they could not secure themselves in the tundra soil. The plants' roots can extend only into the thin layers of sun-warmed soil; they cannot grow deeper into the permafrost.

Marsh marigolds on the Alaskan tundra.

Heather plants, such as bearberry, crow-berry, and mountain cranberry, are well adapted to the tundra climate. These plants have small leathery leaves that help them conserve water during times of drought. As the plants grow, they spread outward, form-ing dense blankets of leaves and stems that warm the air around the plants. On a sunny day, the air next to a plant may be 25 degrees warmer than the surrounding air. The warmth enables the plants to grow faster.

Page 26: Alpine bearberry.
Page 27: Mountain cranberry.

Perhaps the most successful tundra inhabitants are the *Lichens*. Lichens are not plants, but organisms formed by algae and fungi growing together. Over 2,500 types of lichens grow on the dry areas of the tundra soil; some even grow on bare rock. Some lichens look like leafless trees or plastic pot scrubbers. Others look like miniature trumpets or patches of peeling paint.

Orange lichens.

29

During the long arctic winter, lichens lie dormant beneath the tundra snow. They start to grow as soon as the ground begins to thaw. Like tundra plants, lichens do not grow very much during the short arctic summers. A lichen as big as a baseball may be hundreds of years old. The largest lichens have been growing for thousands of years.

Caribou lichens.

The summer vegetation lures many animals to the tundra. One of these summer visitors is the *Caribou*. Caribou spend winters in the forests below the tree line. As spring approaches, enormous herds of caribou, some numbering in the thousands, leave the shelter of the forests and migrate north. The animals roam across the tundra, eating tiny lichens and tender grass and willows. As they forage for food, caribou must always be alert. An unsuspecting caribou is the favorite meal of the tundra wolf.

A caribou herd in summer.
Inset: Foraging on the autumn tundra.

Tundra Wolves, also called arctic wolves, are the supreme hunters of the far north. They have excellent hearing and vision and can smell animals that are more than a mile (1.6 km) away. A large male wolf can be over 6 feet (1.8 m) long and weigh more than 100 pounds (45 kg). Their strong, sleek bodies are made for running. In a sudden burst of speed, they can streak across the tundra at 40 miles (64 km) per hour. They also have exceptional endurance. When they are stalking prey, wolves can trot for hours without a rest.

Tundra wolves live and hunt in family groups called *Packs.* People used to think that wolf packs killed caribou and other animals just for sport. We now know that wolves kill only the animals that they need to eat. What's more, they attack only feeble members of a herd—the young, the sick, and the old. By killing the weakest animals, wolves actually help the caribou herds. Only the strongest caribou survive and produce healthy offspring.

The tundra wolf.

34

Bears, too, inhabit the tundra. After hibernating below the tree line in the winter, the *Barren Ground Grizzly* moves north to dine on the plants and tender berries of the summer. These blond-colored bears are primarily plant eaters, but will also eat fish, lemmings, an occasional wolf cub, and carrion (dead carcasses) left by other animals.

Polar Bears, on the other hand, prefer to eat meat. They live on the edge of the tundra near the Arctic Ocean, where a ready supply of seals, walruses, and fish can be caught. Their long, narrow bodies, powerful hindquarters, and slightly webbed toes make them ideal swimmers, and their thick fur insulates them from the icy Arctic water. These large predators, which can weigh 1,000 pounds (454 kg) or more, seldom wander far inland. When they do, they add berries, carrion, and other tundra animals to their diet.

Two polar bears tread through the snow.
Inset: A mother grizzly and two yearling cubs.

36

Many *Birds,* too, spend summers on the tundra. They migrate from warm southern lands to feed, nest, and raise their young. Millions of swans, ducks, and geese fill the ponds and marshes with ceaseless honking and quacking. Gulls, terns, and other shore birds scurry across the tundra's rocky beaches. Falcons and eagles soar high above the tundra in search of their prey. Smaller songbirds stake out their territories in the low tundra hills, filling the meadows with their various calls.

Most birds hatch in late June, when food on the tundra becomes plentiful. Plants begin to sprout new leaves, and the ponds and lakes are full of fish. Also about this time, an amazing number of *Insects* pervade the tundra. The fields and meadows teem with butterflies, moths, and bumblebees. Thick clouds of mosquitoes and flies swarm after the caribou herds and provide food for the birds and fish.

Canadian geese.

For a time, the tundra blooms with life. But with each passing day, the sun sinks lower and lower in the sky. The meadows turn brown, and the summer visitors begin their journeys to warmer lands. By the end of August, freezing weather has returned.

Soon, the *Arctic Tundra* is gripped by frigid darkness once again.

The tundra in fall, Denali National Park, Alaska.

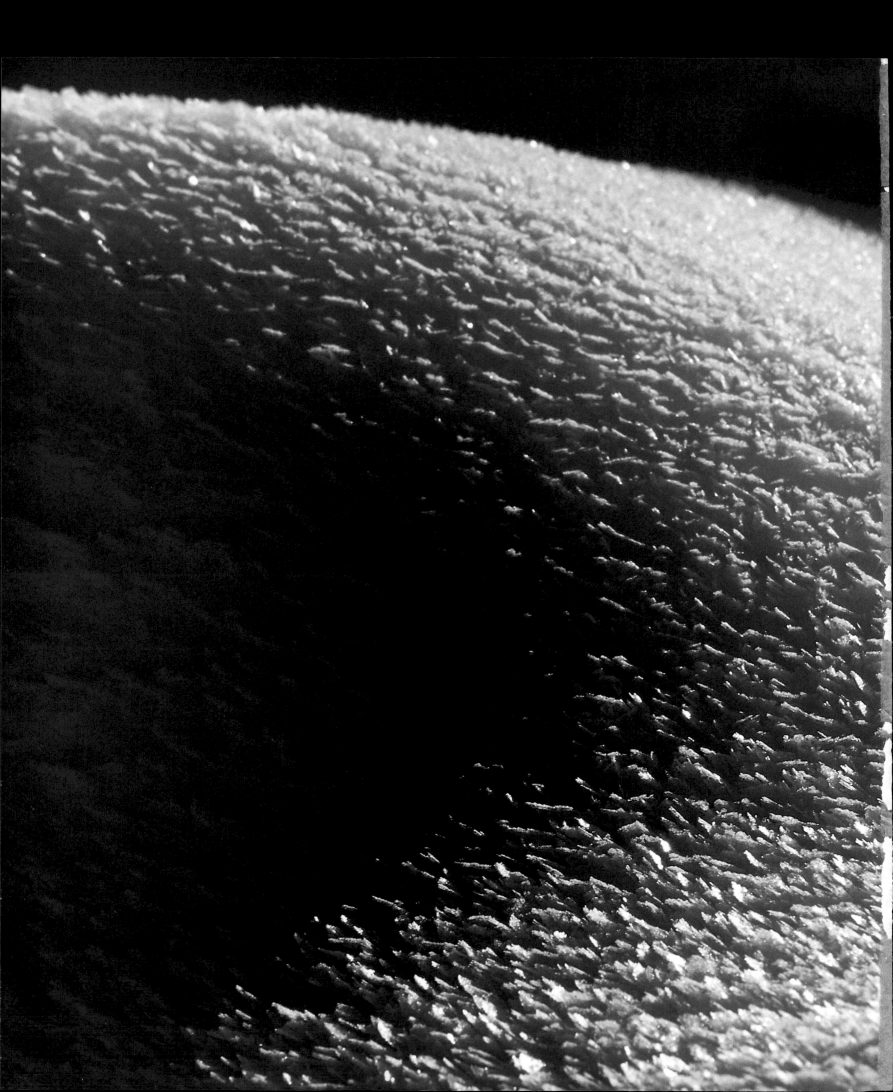